IT'S **NO** FUN
WITHOUT
RUM!

IT'S NO FUN WITHOUT RUM!

50 FABULOUS RECIPES FOR RUM-BASED COCKTAILS, FROM MAI TAI TO MOJITO

DOG 'N' BONE

Published in 2023 by Dog 'n' Bone Books

An imprint of Ryland Peters & Small Ltd
20–21 Jockey's Fields   341 E 116th St
London WC1R 4BW   New York, NY 10029

www.rylandpeters.com

10 9 8 7 6 5 4 3 2 1

A CIP catalog record for this book is available
from the Library of Congress and the British
Library.

UK ISBN: 978-1-912983-81-0
US ISBN: 978-1-912983-78-0

Printed in China

Designer: Geoff Borin

Art Director: Sally Powell

Creative Director: Leslie Harrington

Production Manager: Gordana Simakovic

Contents

Introduction

It's time to dust off your shaker, plug in your blender and gather your limes, because rum is the hottest drink in the world right now! Rum evokes a feeling of escapism like no other spirit and just about everyone needs a vacation don't they? Or at the very least a Mai Tai! Rum has enjoyed a tumultuous history, from its humble origins in the West Indies to its status as the life blood of the Royal Navy and its long-standing love affair with Cuba. It may have a dark past, with tales of devils and pirates and a reputation as the fuel behind revolutionary spirit, but now this fabled drink in all its forms is transforming from grog to a premium spirit that is giving whiskey a run for its money, as well as pulling its weight as the force behind an array of lip-smacking cocktails, both classic and modern. When it comes to rum there's something for everyone. Drunk neat, rum is a marvel. In mixed drinks, it is magical. Here you'll find 50 rum-tastic recipes to take you from bar to beach. Nothing screams tropical holiday like a Piña Colada or Bay Breeze in the hand, and where would we be post work without happy hour icon the Mojito? Elegant cocktail bar menus the world over offer classics like the Dark & Stormy and Dry Daiquiri, but why not try all-too-often overlooked vintage sippers the Air Mail or Rum Runner? You'll find all these here in this carefully curated collection, as well as some fruity punches to get the party started, from Planter's to Passionfruit, and as virtually any cocktail will willingly have its base spirit substituted for the right rum, some conversation starting rum-based twists on your regular gin-based tipples — Rumtini or Tiki Negroni anyone? And finally, some insta-worthy drinks from the Miami Vice to Something Blue will not disappoint those who like their cocktails just a little bit 80s revival! So come cocktail o'clock, whether you find yourself poolside on a lounger, downtown in Havana, or at home, you'll be able to mix, muddle and shake like a pro!

Dry Daiquiri

During Prohibition – when the U.S. imposed 'dry laws' — Facundito Bacardi, the founder of the brand, invited Americans to 'Come to Cuba and bathe in Bacardi rum'. Prohibition may be over but you can still bathe in this delicious Dry Daiquiri.

110 ml/3½ oz. Bacardi

35 ml/1¼ oz. sugar syrup

50 ml/1¾ oz. fresh lime juice

15 ml/½ oz. Campari

a dash of passionfruit syrup

orange twist, to garnish

SERVES 1

Shake all the ingredients in a cocktail shaker with ice cubes and fine-strain into a chilled coupette glass.

Squeeze the zest from the orange twist over the surface of the drink and add it to the glass to garnish. Serve at once.

Hemingway Daiquiri

Legend has it that Ernest Hemingway once consumed 16 of these daiquiris in one sitting — modified from the original recipe by the man himself — in his favourite Havana bar, El Floridita. He's still there, in fact, propping up the bar, immortalized in bronze.

50 ml/1¾ oz. light Puerto Rican-style rum

20 ml/¾ oz. fresh grapefruit juice

10 ml/2 barspoons fresh lime juice

10 ml/2 barspoons maraschino liqueur

lemon peel, to garnish

SERVES 1

Add all the ingredients to a cocktail shaker filled with ice cubes and shake sharply to mix.

Strain into a chilled coupette glass and serve at once garnished with lemon peel.

Strawberry Daiquiri

Whether served on the rocks or frozen, and whether the strawberries are fresh or from the freezer, a strawberry daiquiri is always sweet, refreshing and irresistible.

2 strawberries, plus 1 sliced strawberry, to garnish

125 ml/4 oz. white rum

50 ml/1¾ oz. fresh lime juice

50 ml/1¾ oz. sugar syrup

SERVES 1

Muddle the strawberries in a cocktail shaker, add the other ingredients and shake with ice cubes. Fine-strain into a chilled cocktail glass, garnish with a sliced strawberry fan and serve at once.

Frozen Strawberry Daiquiri: Add all the ingredients to a blender with a handful of ice cubes. Blend at high speed until smooth. Pour into a coupe and serve at once.

The Knickerbocker

The term 'knickerbocker' refers to a New Yorker. While Rat-Packer Sammy Davis Jr. was born in Harlem, his roots came from his African-American and Afro-Cuban parents. Listen to his toe-tapping New York's My Home as you enjoy this tasty punch.

50 ml/1¾ oz. Santa Cruz rum

25 ml/1 oz. orange curaçao

20 ml/¾ oz. fresh lemon juice

15 ml/½ oz. fresh lime juice

fresh raspberries, to garnish

RASPBERRY SYRUP
8 fresh raspberries

150 ml/⅔ cup sugar syrup

SERVES 1

To make the raspberry syrup, put the raspberries in a mixing glass or bowl and press them gently with the back of a spoon to release the juice. Cover with sugar syrup and leave overnight to infuse. Pass the syrup through a fine mesh sieve/strainer and discard the raspberry pulp and seeds.

Add 10 ml/2 barspoons of the raspberry syrup to a cocktail shaker with the rum and curaçao and fill with ice. Squeeze in the juice from the lemon and lime, and drop the spent husks in too. Shake the mixture together.

Strain the drink into a stemmed cocktail glass and serve at once garnished with fresh raspberries.

Commodore Cocktail

Partly set at the Guantanamo Bay Naval Base in Cuba, courtroom drama A Few Good Men is the perfect film to watch as you sip a Commodore. Just try not to choke on the rich, frothy liquid as Jack Nicholson declares, 'You can't handle the truth!'

50 ml/1¾ oz. light puerto rican-style rum

25 ml/1 oz. fresh lemon juice

10 ml/2 barspoons grenadine

10 ml/2 barspoons raspberry syrup (see page opposite)

5 g/1 barspoon caster/ superfine sugar

1 egg white

SERVES 1

Add all ingredients to a cocktail shaker filled with ice cubes and shake sharply to blend and whip up the egg white. Strain into a frosted coupette glass and serve at once while the froth is still at its best.

Twisted Pineapple Frosé

If a Hawaiian luau is your idea of the ultimate summer party, then here is a tropical take on a frosé, perfect for the next time you plan to have some serious fun in the sun.

750 ml/25 oz. rosé wine

250 ml/1 cup fresh pineapple juice

45 ml/1½ oz. white rum

30 ml/1 oz. sugar syrup

30 ml/1 oz. freshly squeezed lime juice

½ a fresh red chilli/chile, deseeded and finely chopped, plus extra to garnish (optional)

pineapple leaf and/or pineapple wedge, to garnish

SERVES 3–4

Pour the rosé wine and pineapple juice into a freezerproof container. Stir to mix and freeze until solid. Remove from the freezer and allow it to defrost for about 35–40 minutes, until you can break it up with a fork but it's still holding plenty of ice crystals.

Scoop into the cup of a blender and add the rum, sugar syrup, lime juice and chilli/chile. Blend for about 30 seconds until foamy and speckled with red chilli/chile. Spoon into serving glasses, add a pineapple leaf and/or a pineapple wedge and a sprinkling of red chilli/chile to garnish (optional).

Serve at once with straws.

Piña Colada

Country singer Garth Brooks sang: 'So bring me two piña coladas; One for each hand; Let's set sail with Captain Morgan; And never leave dry land.' Presumably, he was fantasizing about a Piña Colada in his left hand and a Honey Colada in his right.

120 ml/4 oz. pineapple juice

60 ml/2 oz. white rum

60 ml/2 oz. coconut cream

pineapple wedge, to garnish

SERVES 1

Put all the ingredients into a blender, add a nice scoop of crushed ice and blend. Pour into a glass, garnish with a wedge of pineapple and serve at once.

Honey Colada: For a sweeter version of this drink, add 10 ml/2 barspoons of honey or sugar syrup to the glass after the drink has been poured. Serve at once.

Penzance

Pirates, rum and the sea have been intrinsically linked for centuries. It was only in 1970 that the practice of giving its sailors a daily ration of rum was done away with by the British Royal Navy! Listen to the comic opera Pirates of Penzance to enjoy this cocktail with the appropriate swashbuckling.

40 ml/1½ oz. Bacardi 8-year-old dark rum

10 ml/2 barspoons peach liqueur

25 ml/1 oz. fresh lemon juice

20 ml/¾ oz. bird's eye chilli/chile-infused sugar syrup

4 fresh mint leaves

3 drops of Angostura bitters

ginger beer, to top up

fresh mint sprig, marinated cherry and fresh pineapple wedge, to garnish

SERVES 1

Combine the ingredients in a cocktail shaker; fill up with ice cubes. Shake, then double-strain into a glass. Top up with ginger beer. Fill the glass with ice cubes (beware the fizz), garnish with the mint, cherry and pineapple and serve at once.

Piña Colada Slushie

Conjuring up scenes of beaches with palm trees overhead, the Piña Colada is the drink of choice when lying by the pool. Sadly, this is not always possible — but serving this slushie at home will hopefully transport your mind to sunnier climes.

125 ml/4 oz. coconut milk

125 ml/4 oz. coconut rum such as Malibu

60 ml/2 oz. vodka

375 ml/13 oz. pineapple juice

TO SERVE

200 ml/6¾ oz. pineapple juice (you might not need all of this)

maraschino cocktail cherries and pineapple wedges on a cocktail stick/toothpick, to garnish

freezerproof lidded container, 2 glasses or hollowed out pineapple or coconut shells

SERVES 2

Mix the coconut milk. In the freezerproof container, whisk together the coconut milk, rum, vodka and pineapple juice until well blended. Cover the container with the lid and freeze overnight.

When you are ready to serve, remove the container from the freezer. Do not worry if the mixture has separated, this is normal. Using a fork, crush the mixture to small ice crystals. It should only be semi-frozen due to the vodka and easy to crush. Add the extra pineapple juice slowly and mix to make a slushie consistency — you might not need all of the juice depending on the size of your glass.

Divide the slushie between the glasses or pineapple/coconut shells. Add straws and serve at once, topped with the cherry and wedges of pineapple on a stick.

Cubanada

There's 'nada' more delectable than the sweet taste of maple syrup with golden rum! Those with pronounced oak flavours and full-bodied English Island rums, like ones from Jamaica, will work particularly well in this cocktail. If you use a lighter-bodied rum, cut the maple syrup down to 1 part and add the equivalent amount of sugar syrup.

125 ml/4 oz. rum

50 ml/1¾ oz. maple syrup

50 ml/1¾ oz. fresh lime juice

2 dashes of Angostura bitters

lime slice, to garnish

SERVES 1

Shake all the ingredients with ice and fine-strain into a chilled cocktail glass. Garnish with a thin lime wheel on the rim of the glass and serve at once.

Malecón

Named after an esplanade in Havana, this cocktail was designed by mixologist Erik Lorincz in 2007 for an elegant London cocktail bar to evoke the atmosphere of the Malecón in Havana

30 ml/1 oz. fresh lime juice

2 teaspoons caster/superfine sugar

3 drops of Peychaud's bitters

50 ml/2 oz. Bacardi or other white rum

10 ml/2 barspoons oloroso sherry

15 ml/½ oz. ruby port

SERVES 1

Pre-chill a small cocktail glass with ice. Pour the lime juice over ice in a shaker. Add the rest of the ingredients. Shake. Strain into the glass (having discarded the ice used for chilling). Serve at once with a single cube of ice.

Gum & Tonic

Gum (Gin + Rum) is unusual in that it contains two different spirits; the rum adds base character to the botanical flavours of the gin. Using white or unaged rum results in a lighter drink, whilst an aged rum will add more deep, complex wood and spice notes.

LIGHT GUM & TONIC

30 ml/1 oz. Whittaker's Gin

20 ml/⅔ oz. white rum (Botran Reserva Blanca or Havana Club Anejo 3 Años)

200 ml/6¾ oz. Fever-tree Indian Tonic Water

pineapple flags and lime peel, to garnish

DARK GUM & TONIC

30 ml/1 oz. Sipsmith Gin

20 ml/⅔ oz. Wood's, Pusser's or Lamb's dark rum

200 ml/6¾ oz. Franklin & Sons Natural Light Tonic Water

SERVES 1

Build each drink in an ice-filled glass following the order the ingredients as they are listed. Stir to chill well and serve at once.

Ron Collins

The Ron Collins marches to the beat of its own rum. Based on the Tom Collins but substituting the gin for rum ('ron' in Spanish), it works equally well with light, golden and dark varieties.

125 ml/4 oz. rum

75 ml/2½ oz. sugar syrup

65 ml/2 oz. fresh lime juice

150 ml/5 oz. soda water

3 dashes of Angostura bitters

lime wedge, to garnish

SERVES 1

Pour the first three ingredients over ice into a highball glass. Top up with soda water, then add the Angostura bitters. Garnish with a lime wedge and serve at once.

Ambrosia

Ambrosia was the nectar of the gods and, with Cuba's 160,000 beehives producing lovely, sticky honey, this flavourful drink will leave you buzzing.

125 ml/4 oz. Cuban rum

50 ml/1¾ oz. honey syrup

50 ml/1¾ oz. fresh lime juice

2 dashes of Angostura bitters

orange twist, to garnish

SERVES 1

Shake all the ingredients in a cocktail shaker with ice cubes and fine-strain into a chilled cocktail glass. Squeeze the zest from the orange twist over the surface of the drink, add to the glass as a garnish. Serve at once.

Miami Vice

When you can't decide between two classic rum cocktails, why not combine them? This delicious frozen cocktail consists of two layers: one with the pineapple and coconut creaminess of a Piña Colada, and the other with the strawberry and lime zing of a Daiquiri.

1 x 250-ml/8½-oz. can premixed Strawberry Daiquiri

1 x 250-ml/8½-oz. can premixed Piña Colada

30 ml/1 oz. white rum

SERVES 1

Blend the Strawberry Daiquiri with ice and half of the white rum (15 ml/½ oz.) until it forms a smooth slush. Pour into a hurricane glass. Next, blend the Piña Colada with ice and the rest of the rum (15 ml/½ oz.). Pour into the same hurricane glass on top of the Strawberry Daiquiri slush, creating a layering effect. Serve at once with a straw.

Note: If you prefer, you can make the Strawberry Daiquiri and Piña Colada from scratch using the recipes on pages 11 and 16 and then blend them.

Air Mail

In 1930, the Cuban government started its airmail service. It wasn't long before the Air Mail cocktail appeared in a Bacardi promo leaflet and bartenders attached airmail stamps to the glass as a garnish.

25 ml/1 oz. gold Puerto Rican-style rum

12.5 ml/2½ barspoons fresh lime juice

5 ml/1 barspoon runny honey

chilled Champagne, to top up

Add the rum, lime juice and honey to a cocktail shaker and stir until the honey is dissolved. Add ice and shake to mix. Strain into a Champagne flute, top up with Champagne and serve at once.

SERVES 1

June Bug

Cuba's streets are packed with vintage cars from the 1950s, with the Volkswagen Beetle — or Bug — nipping between Chevrolets, Dodges, Studebakers and Chryslers. Get your engine revving with this bright shooter, which also makes a great long drink. Simply multiply the ingredients by four and serve over ice in a highball glass.

25 ml/1 oz. coconut rum

25 ml/1 oz. Midori melon liqueur

25 ml/1 oz. pineapple juice

a squeeze of fresh lime

SERVES 2

Shake all the ingredients together in a cocktail shaker with ice cubes and strain into a large shot glass. If made properly, the drink will have a nice frothy head. Serve at once.

Paradise Punch

The Caribbean island of Cuba — punctuated by its scattering of archipelagos — is nothing short of paradise. This tropical blend of exotic juices will carry you to utopia, awash with white-sand beaches, swaying palm trees and dive-right-in waters.

1 part tropical juice mix

¼ part dark rum

¼ part white rum

¼ part aged rum

¼ part maraschino liqueur

¼ part lime juice

a dash of grenadine

SERVES 1

Make a mix of your favourite tropical juices; guava, pineapple, mango and passionfruit are a good start. Shake all the ingredients in a cocktail shaker with ice cubes, apart from the grenadine, and pour into a shot glass. Drop a little grenadine into the glass and swirl until you get a perfect sunset effect. Serve at once.

Rum Runner

This cocktail is criminally delicious. During Prohibition, from 1920 to 1933, rum-running — the act of smuggling forbidden alcohol across a border — was rife. It began with cheap Caribbean rum being transported to Florida speakeasies and progressed to Canadian whisky, French Champagne and English gin being delivered to major cities like New York and Boston.

25 ml/1 oz. white rum

25 ml/1 oz. dark rum

fresh juice of 1 lime

a dash of sugar syrup

150 ml/²⁄₃ cup pineapple juice

SERVES 1

Shake all the ingredients sharply over ice cubes in a cocktail shaker and strain into a highball glass filled with crushed ice. Serve at once.

Colonel Beach's Plantation Punch

Created in the 1950s by 'Don the Beachcomber' to be served in his restaurant The Colonel Plantation Beef Steak and Coffee House, this experimental blend of unusual ingredients is pretty punchy.

25 ml/1 oz. gold Cuban rum

50 ml/1¾ oz. gold Jamaican rum

25 ml/1 oz. gold Barbadian rum

25 ml/1 oz. fresh lime juice

50 ml/1¾ oz. ginger beer

50 ml/1¾ oz. pineapple juice

2 dashes of Angostura bitters

2 dashes of Falernum

2 dashes of Pernod

orange slices, cocktail cherries and fresh mint sprigs, to garnish

SERVES 1

Add all the ingredients to a cocktail shaker filled with ice cubes and shake together to mix.

Pour into an ice-filled Tiki mug (if you have one) or glass, and serve at once garnished with an orange slice, cocktail cherry and a mint sprig, held together with a toothpick.

Planter's Punch

While the origins of this drink are disputed, one claim is that it was the creation of a planter's wife, who mixed it to cool down the workers on a Caribbean plantation after a day's toil.

50 ml/1¾ oz. light Puerto Rican-style rum

50 ml/1¾ oz. fresh orange juice

30 ml/1 oz. fresh lemon juice

15 ml/½ oz. grenadine

25 ml/1 oz. soda water

10 ml/2 barspoons dark Jamaican rum

orange slices and cocktail cherries, to garnish

SERVES 1

Add the light rum, orange and lemon juices and grenadine to a cocktail shaker and shake together. Pour into a highball glass filled with crushed ice and top up with soda. Gently pour the dark rum over the surface — it should float naturally on top, while the grenadine should sink to the bottom. Serve at once garnished with an orange slice and a cocktail cherry, held together with a toothpick.

Passionfruit Punch

If there's one thing Cuban music inspires, it's passion. Whether it's rumba, Afro-Cuban jazz, son cubano or salsa, each beat is sure to get your feet tapping and your hips swaying. The Passionfruit Punch will certainly inspire your thirst for rhythm... plus quench your dry mouth once you've built up a sweat.

300 ml/10 oz. white rum

150 ml/5 oz. passionfruit pulp (from about 6 large ripe passionfruit)

150 ml/5 oz. fresh orange juice

600 ml/20 oz. clear sparkling lemonade

SERVES 6

Put the rum, passionfruit pulp and orange juice in a large jug/pitcher and chill for an hour. Half-fill six tall glasses with ice, add the rum and fruit juice mixture and top up with lemonade. Serve at once.

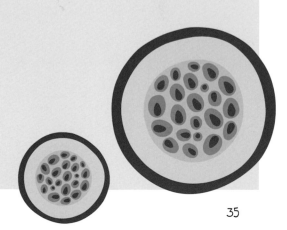

Something Blue

A tropical tipple with both an exotic fruitiness and a sweet nuttiness; its alluring colour transporting you to the shoreline of a sun-kissed island, the sea lapping upon the golden sands.

30 ml/1 oz. coconut rum

25 ml/¾ oz. vanilla vodka

45 ml/1½ oz. pineapple juice

10 ml/2 tsp Amaretto

15 ml/½ oz. lime juice

a float (approx. 10 ml/ 2 tsp) of blue Curaçao

pineapple wedges, to garnish

SERVES 1

Add the ingredients, apart from the blue Curaçao, to a cocktail shaker with ice cubes and shake vigorously. Pour into an ice-filled hurricane glass, or similar. Pour 10 ml/2 tsp blue Curaçao down the inside of the glass. The Curaçao will sink, creating the layered effect. Garnish with pineapple wedges and serve at once.

Rumtini

This Martini variation simply uses unaged rum instead of gin or vodka. You can use your own preferred ratio of rum to vermouth and mix it however you like, although stirring is often more sympathetic to the rum's underlying character.

50 ml/1¾ oz. unaged rum

10 ml/½ oz. dry vermouth

twist of lime peel and grated nutmeg, to garnish (optional)

SERVES 1

Stir ingredients in a mixing glass with ice cubes before straining into a small, stemmed wine glass. Garnish with a twist of lime peel and a pinch of grated nutmeg and serve at once.

Spice Island

This drink pairs the deep complexity of red vermouth and spiced rum with the woody notes of aged rum.

30 ml/1 oz. aged rum

10 ml/½ oz. red vermouth

10 ml /½ oz. Cinnabar or other spiced rum

twist of orange peel, to garnish

Add the ingredients to a cocktail shaker and shake vigorously with ice cubes. Strain into a tall, stemmed glass, garnish with a twist of orange peel and serve at once.

SERVES 1

Dark & Stormy

Dark & Stormy is hailed as the national drink of Bermuda. Although its name sounds like trouble it is refreshing served over ice. Homemade ginger beer gives this drink a zestier flavour.

60 ml/2 oz. Goslings Black Seal rum or similar

ginger beer, to top up

lime wedges, to serve

SERVES 1

Fill a chilled glass with crushed ice. Pour in the rum and top with ginger beer. Finish with a squeeze of lime and serve.

Dark & Strawmy: Muddle (squash) 2 hulled and sliced strawberries in a glass. Add crushed ice and finish as above. Serve at once.

Bay Breeze

This uncomplicated and refreshing drink is an International Bartenders Association (IBA) official cocktail. (Pictured on page 2.)

50 ml/1¾ oz. golden rum

100 ml/3½ oz. cranberry juice

50 ml/1¾ oz. pineapple juice

lime wedge, to garnish

SERVES 1

Add all the ingredients to a cocktail shaker filled with ice cubes, shake and strain into a highball glass filled with ice. Garnish with a lime wedge and serve at once.

Mai Tai

There's great debate as to who first concocted the Mai Tai — either 'Don the Beachcomber' or 'Trader Vic'. Trader Vic spent much time in Cuba refining his bartending skills and knowledge of rum, while Don the Beachcomber travelled around many Caribbean islands before opening his first bar in Hollywood. Regardless of who dreamt up the Mai Tai, they probably both agreed that it tastes 'very good', which is its Tahitian translation.

100 ml/3½ oz. gold rum

50 ml/1¾ oz. orange Curaçao

25 ml/1 oz. orgeat (almond) syrup

50 ml/1¾ oz. fresh lime juice

a dash of Angostura bitters

25 ml/1 oz. dark rum

fresh mint sprig, to garnish

SERVES 1

Shake the first 5 ingredients in a cocktail shaker with ice cubes and strain into a large rocks glass over cubed ice. Gently float the dark rum over the surface and then garnish with the mint sprig. Serve at once.

Mojito

One of the world's most popular cocktails, the fresh, minty Mojito was famously enjoyed by novelist Ernest Hemingway at La Bodeguita del Medio bar in Havana, a bar still frequented by many cocktail drinkers today.

8 fresh mint leaves

125 ml/4 oz. Cuban rum

50 ml/1¾ oz. fresh lime juice

50 ml/1¾ oz. sugar syrup

mint sprigs, to garnish

SERVES 1

Gently muddle the mint leaves in a large highball glass. Add the other ingredients and swizzle with crushed ice. Garnish with a mint sprig and serve at once.

Note: The mint garnish is so important with this drink. Use a healthy bushel of mint to make the drink look great and to encourage a fragrant aroma.

Rum 'n' Rosé on the Rocks

This laid-back drink has a distinct feel of the Deep South, worthy of sipping on any porch swing.

30 ml/1 oz. dark rum

15 ml/½ oz. rosé vermouth

75 ml/2½ oz. bottled French peach juice or purée

50 ml/1¾ oz. fruity rosé wine, well-chilled

1–2 teaspoons sugar syrup, to taste (optional)

chilled soda water, to top up

a slice of fresh peach and a fresh mint sprig, to garnish

ice cubes

SERVES 1

Put a rocks glass in the freezer for 5 minutes to frost. Remove it from the freezer and fill with ice cubes. Add the rum, rosé vermouth, peach juice and cold rosé to the glass. Stir to mix and then add 1–2 teaspoons of sugar syrup to taste. Garnish with a slice of fresh peach and a fresh mint sprig. Serve at once.

Cuba Libre

Translated as 'Free Cuba', the Cuba Libre is said to have originated in 1900 in Havana when Captain Russell of the U.S. Army ordered a Bacardi rum with a Coca-Cola and a slice of lime to celebrate the U.S. victory over Spain in Cuba. He raised his glass and toasted: 'Por Cuba libre!'

125 ml/4 oz. Cuban rum

35 ml/1¼ oz. fresh lime juice

250 ml/1 cup carbonated cola

lime wedges, to garnish

SERVES 1

Build all the ingredients over ice cubes in a highball glass, garnish with two lime wedges and serve at once.

Officer's Nightcap

Fancy a warming nightcap? This sophisticated tipple will not disappoint. Pimento Dram liqueur is made by soaking allspice berries in a rum base, the result is best described as a combination of cinnamon, nutmeg and clove — what's not to like?

25 ml/1 oz. fresh lime juice

10 ml/2 barspoons Velvet Falernum

15 ml/½ oz. agave syrup

15 ml/½ oz. Ron Zacapa dark rum

60 ml/2 oz. apple juice

10 ml/2 barspoons Pimento Dram liqueur

lime twist and cinnamon sticks, to garnish

SERVES 1

First, fill a highball glass with ice cubes and set aside. Add all the ingredients to a shaker. Give a quick stir and top up with ice. Shake. Strain any melted water from the glass but leave the ice in it. Strain the cocktail into the glass, garnish with the lime twist and cinnamon stick and serve at once.

The Lounger

The name of this cocktail incorporates the names of the ingredients, rather than referring to your likely activities after you've drunk a few, by the way. It will work nicely with light or dark rum.

25 ml/1 oz. fresh lime juice

25 ml/1 oz. vanilla-infused rum

25 ml/1 oz. ginger cordial

¼ teaspoon sugar syrup

cocktail cherry, to garnish

SERVES 1

Measure the lime, rum, ginger and sugar syrup into a cocktail shaker. Add a couple of ice cubes, replace the lid and shake hard. Pour into a cocktail glass and add a cocktail cherry if you want a touch of extra sweetness. Serve at once

Note: Golden rum can be infused with all manner of delicious delicacies. Make your own spiced rum by popping a cinnamon stick, cloves, star anise and orange zest into a bottle of golden rum and leaving to impart flavour for at least 24 hours.

Anejo Highball

This drink was created in 2000 by master mixologist Dale DeGroff, rum, lime and Curaçao being the holy trinity of Caribbean cocktails in his opinion. Garnished with a lime wheel and orange slice to give a nod to the ingredients within the glass, this is the perfect refresher to cool down with on a hot summer day.

100 ml/3½ oz. Cuban rum

50 ml/1¾ oz. orange Curaçao

50 ml/1¾ oz. fresh lime juice

2 dashes of Angostura bitters

200 ml/7 oz. ginger beer

lime wheel and orange slice, to garnish

SERVES 1

Add the first 4 ingredients to a highball glass filled with ice. Stir well, top up with ginger beer and garnish with a lime wheel and orange slice. Serve at once.

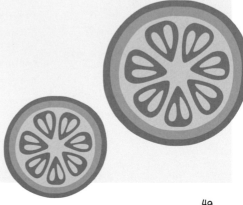

Swizzle

The most supreme swizzle can be accomplished with a pronged wooden swizzle stick hailing from the Caribbean island of Martinique. To swizzle effectively, use both hands to spin the stick between your palms as quickly as possible.

juice of ½ a lime

3 drops of The Bitter Truth Repeal Bitters

10 ml/2 barspoons Pimento Dram liqueur

50 ml/2 oz. Ron Zacapa dark rum

lime twist and grated tonka bean, to garnish

Combine all the ingredients in a highball glass. Fill three-quarters of the way up with crushed ice. Give a good swizzle. Top up with more crushed ice. Garnish with a lime twist and a few gratings of tonka bean and serve at once.

SERVES 1

Queen's Park Swizzle

This drink is a kind of hybrid between the Daiquiri and the Mojito. In 1946, this enlivening drink was described as 'the most delightful form of amnesia given out today'.

50 ml/1¾ oz. Guyanese rum (try El Dorado 12-year)

20 ml/¾ oz. fresh lime juice

15 ml/½ oz. dark sugar syrup

2 dashes of Angostura bitters

5 fresh mint leaves, plus a mint sprig, to garnish

SERVES 1

Add the rum, lime juice, sugar syrup, Angostura bitters and mint leaves to a highball glass filled with crushed ice. Swizzle by placing a barspoon or small whisk into the glass and swizzling between the palms of your hands until frost appears on the outside of the glass. Serve at once garnished with a mint sprig.

Pinkie Swizzle

This sparkling rum swizzle reinvented is an ice-cold, lip-tingling treat with the addition or rosé wine.

40 ml/1½ oz. 100% pomegranate juice

30 ml/1 oz. Bacardi or other white rum

10 ml/¼ oz. sugar syrup

60 ml/2 oz. rosé Prosecco, well-chilled

pomegranate seeds, to garnish

crushed ice

SERVES 1

Combine the pomegranate juice, rum and syrup in a cocktail shaker with ice cubes and shake until chilled. Strain into a crushed-ice-filled rocks glass and pour in the Prosecco. Garnish with pomegranate seeds and serve at once.

Watermelon Swizzle: Replace the pomegranate juice with fresh watermelon juice and a squeeze of lime. Garnish with a wedge of watermelon and a slice of fresh chilli/chile. Serve at once.

Shelter from the Storm

The original Dark & Stormy cocktail is one of the few trademarked cocktails, and should 'legally' be made with Gosling's Black Seal Rum. This variation adds orange notes from the Curaçao and almond from the orgeat almond-flavoured syrup, and can be made with any aged or dark rum. If you want to 'shelter from the storm', enjoy during the months of June to November — hurricane season.

100 ml/3½ oz. aged or dark rum

25 ml/1 oz. orange Curaçao or Cointreau

25 ml/1 oz. orgeat (almond) syrup

50 ml/1¾ oz. fresh lime juice

200 ml/7 oz. ginger beer

sliced ginger (optional) and lime wedge, to garnish

SERVES 1

Add the first 4 ingredients to a large highball glass filled with ice cubes and stir. Top up with the ginger beer and garnish with a slice of ginger and a lime wedge. Serve at once.

Hurricane

This cocktail was created by Pat O'Brien in his New Orleans tavern in the 1940s. Try to use proper passionfruit syrup instead of hurricane mix.

50 ml/2 oz. dark rum

25 ml/1 oz. fresh lemon juice

25 ml/1 oz. passion fruit syrup

passion fruit juice (optional)

passion fruit seeds, to garnish

SERVES 1

Add all the ingredients to a cocktail shaker filled with ice cubes and shake vigorously to mix.

Strain into a hurricane glass filled with crushed ice, top up with passionfruit juice, if using, and serve at once garnished with passion fruit seeds.

Tiki Negroni

Picking up on the Tiki trend, rum and gin are combined here to create a cocktail full of plump tropical notes with a balanced sweetness that will be a hit with the legions of Negroni fans out there already.

25 ml/1 oz. Citadelle Gin

25 ml/1 oz. red vermouth

25 ml/1 oz. Campari

25 ml/1 oz. Plantation Pineapple Rum

3–4 dashes Angostura Bitters

lime wheel, small pineapple wedge and pineapple leaves, to garnish

SERVES 1

Add the ingredients to an ice-filled cocktail shaker and shake vigorously.

Fine-strain into an ice-filled rocks glass and garnish with a lime wheel, lime, pineapple wedge and leaves and serve at once.

Kingston Negroni

This is a rum-based version of the Negroni that marries the beloved Italian cocktail with the warm, intense and gently sweet character of rum. It is named after the capital city of Jamaica, Kingston. The drink works with a variety of rums, but the best results come from using a Jamaican pot-still rum such as Smith & Cross, which is packed full of complex flavours.

25 ml/1 oz. Smith & Cross Jamaican Rum

25 ml/1 oz. red vermouth

25 ml/1 oz. Campari

flamed orange twist, to garnish

SERVES 1

Add the ingredients to an ice-filled mixing glass and stir. Strain into an ice-filled rocks glass and finish and garnish with a flamed orange twist. Serve at once.

Rum Sombrero

Tia Maria is a rum-based coffee liqueur with a history dating back to the 17th century. Legend has it that a beautiful Spanish aristocrat fled Jamaica due to the colonial wars, leaving behind her possessions. Her maid saved a jewellery box containing a pair of black pearl earrings and a recipe for a liqueur, which was later named after her.

100 ml/3½ oz. rum

50 ml/1¾ oz. Tia Maria

25 ml/1 oz. espresso

a dash of dark sugar syrup

50 ml/1¾ oz. double/heavy cream, lightly whipped

coffee beans or pinch of ground cinnamon, to garnish

Shake the first 4 ingredients in a cocktail shaker with ice cubes and strain into a chilled cocktail glass. Float the lightly whipped cream on top and garnish with three coffee beans or a pinch of ground cinnamon. Serve at once.

SERVES 1

Graham Cracker Crunch

A sweet and spicy cocktail designed to emulate the classic American snack. RumChata is a rum-based, cream liqueur flavoured with cinnamon and spices.

20 ml/1 oz. RumChata cream liqueur

20 ml/1 oz. blanco tequila

20 ml/1 oz. cinnamon whiskey

cinnamon and sugar, for the rim of the glass and to garnish (optional)

SERVES 1

Coat the rim of a cocktail glass with cinnamon sugar (if using). Add the ingredients to a cocktail shaker with ice cubes and shake vigorously. Strain into the sugar-rimmed glass. Sprinkle with a little extra cinnamon and serve at once.

Caribbean Flip

A flip is a type of mixed drink dating back to 1695, although it's evolved a lot since then. This Caribbean version is rich, luxurious and warming. Your taste buds will certainly flip with delight.

100 ml/3½ oz. dark or light rum, as preferred

25 ml/1 oz. orange Curaçao

50 ml/1¾ oz. dark sugar syrup

75 ml/2½ oz. double/heavy cream

2 dashes of Angostura bitters

a pinch of ground cinnamon

1 small egg yolk

cinnamon stick and freshly grated nutmeg, to garnish

SERVES 1

Shake all the ingredients very hard with ice for at least 30 seconds; the harder you shake, the lighter the texture will be. Strain into a chilled wine glass and garnish with a long stick of cinnamon and some freshly grated nutmeg to serve.

Mon Cheri

Vinegar-based cocktails are a fashionable favourite on the London cocktail circuit and rightly so. The vinegar cuts through the sweetness of the cocktail, adding a delicious sweet and sour flavour. You may have difficulty stopping at one glass! This one is for all those chocolate and cherry lovers out there.

50 ml/2 oz. Grand Marnier

25 ml/1 oz. rum

2 tablespoons finely grated dark/bittersweet chocolate

15 ml/½ oz. cherry liqueur

2 barspoons cider vinegar

SERVES 1

Shake all the ingredients together and serve with ice.

Mon Cheri Mozart: If you fancy this cocktail without the sour edge of the cider vinegar, replace it with 2 barspoons of dark chocolate liqueur, such as Mozart. It will taste like the Mon Cheri chocolates in a glass!

Recipe credits

BEN REED
Air Mail
Bay Breeze
Colonel Beach's
    Plantation Punch
Commodore Cocktail
Cuba Libre
Dark & Strawmy
Hemingway Daiquiri
Hurricane
Mojito
Piña Colada
Honey Colada
Planter's Punch
Queen's Park Swizzle
Rum Runner
The Knickerbocker

MICHAEL BUTT
Ambrosia
Anejo Highball
Caribbean Flip
Cubanada
Dry Daiquiri
June Bug
Mai Tai
Paradise Punch

Ron Collins
Rum Sombrero
Shelter from the Storm
Strawberry Daiquiri
Frozen Strawberry
    Daiquiri

**DAVID T SMITH &
KELI RIVERS**
Graham Cracker
    Crunch
Gum & Tonic
Kingston Negroni
Miami Vice
Rumtini
Something Blue
Spice Island
Tiki Negroni

**FROM *THE AMERICAN
BAR* BY WILLIAM
YEOWARD**
Malecon
Officer's Nightcap
Penzance
Swizzle

JULIA CHARLES
Pinkie Swizzle
Rum 'n' Rosé on the
    Rocks
Twisted Pineapple Frosé
Watermelon Swizzle

LOUISE PICKFORD
Passionfruit Punch

JANET SAWYER
The Lounger

URSULA FERRIGNO
Mon Cheri
Mon Cheri Mozart

VALERIE AIKMAN-SMITH
Dark & Stormy

HANNAH MILES
Piña Colada Slushie

Photography credits

GAVIN KINGCOMB pages 20 and 50; ALEX LUCK pages 15, 19, 23, 27, 37, 39, 45, 53, 56, 58 and 60; WILLIAM LINGWOOD pages 2, 13, 16, 28, 32, 43, 46 and 55; MARTIN NORRIS pages 24, 25, 30 and 61; JAN BALDWIN page 63; STEVE PAINTER age 48; ERIN KUNKEL age 40; ADDIE CHINN page 8.